CRUMBLED
A Place
for Broken People

CRUMBLED
A Place
for Broken People

AMANDA SCHAEFER

ISBN: 978-0-578-50214-4 (Paperback)
ISBN: 978-0-578-50215-1(eBook)

Printed by Ingram Spark, in the United States of America.
First Printing 2019.

Cover and book design by Jackson Schaefer

For information contact Footbridge Publishing House
www.footbridgepublishinghouse.com

This book is dedicated to the remnant in my family, those who believe in God. No matter what happens in the Bible, there is always a remnant. My fellow believers, my Mom and Dad, my Son and Daughter and my Son in law, thank you for your unending support and encouragement. I need you and appreciate you all as much as I love you!

TABLE OF CONTENTS

FOREWARD

If your life is problem-free or anything less than perfect, you probably don't need this book. But if you know what it is to struggle, if you're aware of your own brokenness, if you could use a well-timed word of encouragement, you've come to the right place.

Amanda Schaefer is my friend. She is an Encourager with a capital "E." Best of all, she is human: she doesn't hide the bumps and bruises she has accumulated on the road of life. And every scar comes with a story of God's redeeming grace.

Amanda loves Jesus, and she loves people. She possesses an uncanny knack for sensing what God is whispering to her heart and a fervent desire to do what He says.

I'm thankful for Amanda's obedience because God has used her stories - whether on her blog, on the platform, in writing or over an early-morning cup of coffee - to encourage my heart. I come away from our times together with a smile on my face and a spring in my step. Amanda is one of those people who drinks so deeply of Jesus that He can't help but spill over into the lives of of those she touches.

This is a book that will challenge and encourage you. It is more than a compilation of Amanda's stories; it's an opportunity to see how God can and will work in the life of anyone who is open to His leading. It's also an opportunity to think deeply about your own life and gain a sense of where God might be leading you.

I urge you to do more than read this book. I encourage you to prayerfully interact with it by thinking about the questions at the end of each chapter and writing down your thoughts and dreams. And I challenge you to act on what God reveals to you as you draw near to Him through this book.

So go ahead. Turn the page and join Amanda as she shares her adventures with God. Chances are, you'll see yourself in some of her stories. Better yet, you'll see the love and grace of God that are available to all of us when we bring our brokenness to Him.

-Tracey Somerville

INTRODUCTION

When I first became a Christian, I was attending the church I had grown up in. I hadn't gone there in years. I returned when I moved back into the area. But I found it difficult to stay there after a dramatic personal encounter with Jesus. You see, I had wanted to be perfect there. I felt the need to hide my brokenness.

I didn't see any examples of vulnerable, struggling people and indeed, no leaders dared to show their weaknesses. I spent the majority of my life living cracked, scarred and notably broken. From a young age, I began pretending that everything was perfect. But nothing is perfect in this world. Nothing but Jesus.

Don't get me wrong, I am not condemning that specific church. I am condemning the Church at large. I am challenging the truth of what we have turned Church into. I am condemning men and church. We are supposed to be the church. We are supposed to be the body of Christ. How can we be a body if everyone wants to be the same part? How can we function? How can we reach out to love the world around us?

I am condemning our self-doubt and our lack of identity. I am condemning our fear that we are not enough and its insatiable call for us to continually look polished and happy and wealthy and skinny and (insert unattainable adjective here). All the while we are letting our loved ones, our children, our parents, our very own hearts, slip into an abyss of fear and failure and disconnection and depression. We have no idea who we are anymore unless we read it on a billboard or see it in an Instagram post.

The world tells us to apply filters to make ourselves look younger and more interesting. Let me say something, God made you UNIQUE. There is no one on the planet like you. You were intricately planned and created. You are beautiful beyond description, and you are killing yourself trying to be just like everyone else. You are containing yourself to blend in. I am here to tell you to stop it! Stand up! Speak out! Be who you were made to be! Do what you were made to do! True happiness cannot be achieved by pretending.

We all have crummy moments. We all fall and fail and doubt and lose. We need to be real with each other. We have to stop trying to convince people that we are okay all of the time. We need to share our messes. We need to share while we are amid difficulty and we need to share when we have made it through to the other side and survived it. We basically need to share period!

This book includes some crummy, messy, and gut-wrenching stories. It also contains some fantastic, uplifting, and miraculous stories. That balance is what Christianity is genuinely like. It is what life on this side of heaven is going to be. And even in the tough times, there are always poignant glimpses of who God is in our troubles with us. You see I go through bad things, but I never go through them alone. For me to tell you that being a Christian is perfect is wrong. I am depriving you of something Jesus died to give you, "hope." There is hope in the darkest places, and His name is Jesus.

Several years ago I clearly felt God nudging me to start a new blog. I had written a blog before chronicling my training and experiences for a missions trip to Malawi, Africa. At times I had thought it a great success having been read by more than three thousand people. But the blog God was asking me to write this time was different. Over some time reading His word, praying and journaling I concluded that I was being prompted to write a daily blog. This was to be done first thing in the morning without much preparation, just a vulnerable, honest stream of my thoughts. I agreed and set up the new blog. Little did I know that only a short time later my entire world would begin to fall apart!

I believe that capturing those broken moments was God's plan for me. As I wrote each day, I was able to not only share the situations and circumstances that I found myself in, but I was also able to explain how God showed me His character, His love, and His provision during the bleakest of times.

I poured out my heart onto those pages and I waivered some days to push the "publish" button. I was sending my messy life out into the unlimited internet in such a raw and imperfect way. Growth continued on, and I kept my promise to write daily.

One day a leader at my church asked me out to lunch. I had done ministry with her before and gladly accepted. What she said to me at that dining table rocked my heart. She suggested that I no longer share such intimate details in my writing. She went on to express that many saw me as a leader, and because of that position, it was my responsibility to appear healthy. She also indicated that I could describe God in ways that would be less explicit and could, therefore, bring Him more glory. She had a great desire to reach the unchurched and thought that this type of personal sharing deterred such opportunities. I left that conversation in a state of disappointment and felt inadequate. But after some prayer do you know what I did? I wrote a new entry, and I explained what she had said to me. I was kind and respectful and kept her anonymous, but I disagreed with her unrequested advice.

Listening to well-intentioned people's wisdom instead of seeking God's wisdom is dangerous. I could have easily given up what I was doing and tried a new approach, but if I had I never would have reached the thousands of people who have read my blog (more than 31,000 readers at this time and all over the world I might add).

If I had given up and given in, I wouldn't have ministered to hundreds if not thousands of other people over the years through speaking engagements, writing opportunities, and personal life situations. If I had failed to follow God's directive, I wouldn't have started a publishing company with my son, or have written this book, or the others I am working on at this very moment.

People mean well, but let me tell you a secret, that woman is not even in leadership anymore. We all need to trust our own experiences and follow our own dreams. I am so glad that I was willing to offer up my broken pieces over the years to others who were in the midst of pain and trouble. It has been my own heart's biggest blessing.

Jesus offered up His life to be broken and poured out for us all. Isn't it only fitting that we as His followers should do the same? The only way that we can share the love and grace that we have received is, to be honest, vulnerable, available and willing to open up and share the reality of our lives with others. The highest command in the Bible is to love God and to love others. Sharing your struggles and experiences is the only way to really do that. First, we must share with God. He already knows what we are going through, but His desire is to be invited into the circumstance with us. He won't barge in, we must ask Him. He wants to be near to us, and He wants to turn our weak places into a strong foundation, into a platform for sharing the love of the gospel with others. Second, we must share our inabilities and our difficulties with other people to bridge the gap in our lives and to provide a real trust and connection with which to love them.

Do not be ashamed of your life! Stop hiding your mistakes and rewriting your failures. Don't bury your trauma or gloss-over your struggles. Instead, I challenge you to go around breaking off pieces of yourself and sharing them with people. We are all like a loaf of bread. If we are not broken, we cannot be shared. Would you rather become hardened without sharing any of yourself, or share yourself and help others? And if you decide to share yourself, you will find that you never run out of pieces, there will always be bread left to offer to feed another hungry soul. If we are all doing it right, we will feed each other! The real church is meant to be lived together. A community is a part of how we were intended to live. Jesus showed us the way, He gave us example after example of how to live and how to love. We may be the only example of His kingdom that someone else might ever encounter.

PART ONE

DIGGING A WELL
FOR NINETY DAYS

So many things happened that year. As I looked through the photos in my hands, I realized that it would be impossible to think of them all. Each thing that came to mind was particular, whether good or bad, somehow necessary to bring me to this very moment. My life is good, excellent, but there was one thing that happened a few years ago that changed my life forever. Most people saw it on the outside, but it began as a change within.

I lost over thirty pounds and three dress sizes that year. I should start by saying that I had been diagnosed with three autoimmune diseases. Each one added limitations, difficulties and another fifteen pounds to my ever-growing body. When I was in my prime, I could wear anything I wanted and eat anything I wanted, and I usually did both.

After having gained so much weight, I felt lost, depressed and unlovable. I had tried everything I could think of to lose weight, but nothing seemed to work.

Over the years God has completely healed me of the symptoms of those diseases, but the weight seemed to hang on like a curse. Then one day I clearly heard God say, "Dig a well for Ninety days". What, I wondered, did that mean? As I prayed and listened, I began to hear more. God was challenging me to live differently for ninety days.

During that time I promised Him to eat healthier, drink more water, and spend even more time with Him. Typically, if anyone asked me to do something for three months, it would have sounded too overwhelming, but I eagerly answered yes. I knew somehow that this was for my own good. In the past, even doing a short diet seemed impossible, but I must have been ready for a change. And after ninety days of doing something different I found that it had become a lifestyle.

God gives us perfect direction through His word as to how we should live. Some things seem impossible, but when God gives you a strategy, He makes a way where there had been no way by your own ability or through your personal planning. I began the ninety days by making changes in every aspect of my life. As I started to eat healthy food, I realized that I didn't seem to miss the bad stuff that much. Drinking more water felt great. It was as if I had been dehydrated for my entire life and

4

somehow had never known it. Spending more time with God was difficult, as I already got up at five a.m. to start my day with Him. What I found myself doing was being more open to experiencing God in new ways. I spent more time in worship, and I spent a lot more time listening for His guidance.

As the months began to pass my body began to change. I not only got skinnier, but my hair and skin started to look healthier as well. It took losing two dress sizes before other people seemed to take note of what was happening on my outside. When they inquired, it gave me an opportunity to tell them about what was happening on my inside. Leave it to God to provide me with a new avenue to speak about my relationship with Him and His perfect love for me.

Another significant thing happened when God set this choice before me; I got to choose a blessing instead of accepting a curse. In daring to walk somewhere that seemed impossible, God had more in store for me. It was as if I had been standing at a crossroads, to the left was my current life which was very good, but to the right was what I would need for the next season of my life. As I stood at that place and chose to follow God's direction, something that had always had a strong hold over me, broke. I stepped away from under its weight, and with that very first step into the unknown, I left it behind forever. When I believed my Father in heaven over the clamor of the world, over my own voice, over the enemy's lies, I was already free, I just didn't see it yet. I had lost all of the weight in the spiritual realm way before I got to see the results in the physical world. The weight loss happened as soon as I chose to honestly believe that God could do what had been impossible for me to do on my own. I had thought that I believed that God could do anything about everything, but this was one of those subtle little lies that had wiggled its way into my heart.

Having doctors tell me that I had these illnesses and that they had specific symptoms and effects on my body and my life had restricted my belief in this area that God could do anything more. It was at the moment that His voice interrupted me while I was doing something else, it was then that I was ready to hear what He had to say. It was when I chose to listen that everything changed.

Not only did God have a plan for me to get physically, spiritually and emotionally healthier, but this was a preparation for what would come next. About a month into this lifestyle change, a friend of mine from church contacted me privately on Facebook. It seems she had thought that I needed to meet another friend of hers who went to another one of our Church's campuses. I was intrigued and agreed, and we ended up having breakfast together. To make a long story short, this person I "had to meet," well, I really did need to meet her. She was having a Women's teaching event and somehow by the time we were done our morning together, I was sent home to "pray about sharing my full testimony" at this event.

Let me backup a bit and let you see the timeline which God had laid out in front of me. When I started the ninety days of "digging a well," I also wrote out my full testimony to be shared in about thirty minutes time. Why had I done this? This was the second thing that I had heard God prompting me to do in faith and obedience after agreeing to dig the well. I decided to speak and when I did found out that the event date was the day after my ninety days would be over! Amazing timing right?

I was about to share with the world things that no one had ever known about my life (and there was a lot of deep dark things to talk about). As a matter of fact, I had to share with my parents and kids first. Thankfully, the kids are adults now, so it was appropriate to tell them. Letting loose of the things that had happened to me and the horrible choices that I had made as life went along didn't break me, it freed me. I no longer carried the shame. I had been redeemed.

When I arrived at the Women's event one of my best friends quickly pointed to a beautiful stone well on the edge of the property. I posed for a picture next to it. Not only did the Well stand for what God had asked of me, but when I had asked God how He wanted me to share at this event, He had guided me to the story of the woman at the well from the book of John in chapter four. Amazingly I had never seen myself anywhere in that story, but seeing as I had had two husbands before meeting Jesus, it was the perfect avenue to use.

Indeed I WAS the woman at the well. We never get to see in the story how she got to be that woman or why she had made those bad choices. What we do get to see in this Biblical story is that Jesus met her there regardless of what she had done or what had been done to her. Jesus loved her and took the time to meet with her to offer her His living water, precisely as He had done with me.

The woman who held this event and I have since become friends. I love to talk to her and to pray with her. She is a great encouragement to me. It is crazy to think that we haven't always known each other as it feels as if we have. Crazier yet, that we met in such a unique way. I will be forever grateful that my friend Meenu heard God clearly and was obedient to connect us!

I decided to write about my weight loss because so many people have asked me what I did to lose the weight. I know some people who take cleanses and supplements, and I think it's tremendous and I wish them much success. I exercise and continue to make healthy choices, but I want to convey that there was more than a physical ailment going on in my life. In such cases, there is more work to do than just eat differently.

A change in my heart needed to happen before the difference in my body could occur. That is true of many trying to lose weight. I have been through some dangerous and difficult things in my life, but I wouldn't change a thing because I learned how to find pure joy in the Lord no matter what my circumstances. I have learned how to appreciate

This year was also the Year of Jubilee, which only occurs every fifty years. At my age, this is the only Jubilee year I will see on this side of heaven. The year of Jubilee is the year that all debts are forgiven. God established this for all of His people as a year of freedom and joy. I can move into the next year knowing that it too will be full of blessing, not because of what I do or what I have, but because of who I am. I am the daughter of the One True King, and that alone is the best thing that I could ever be, the best gift I could ever receive, the best place I could ever find myself in - smack dab in the middle of His perfect Love!

This morning I woke up and it was a new year. Unlike many, last night I was asleep by nine o'clock. This morning I took my dog for a walk very early, and the earth was quiet. It was strange not to see a single neighbor's light on. Not one car drove by on the road. Outside Christmas lights blinked on and off and the mist of a thick fog had fallen all around me. I knew that I would be heading back into the house to write. "Thank You" I whispered into the still morning air. "I love You" I continued, breathing in a deep, fresh breath. I exhaled it slowly into the world around me.

All of this is connected. There is a timeline to my life, to your life, God has a plan... At that moment, standing there in the quiet, I saw it all from His perspective. Last year was just a blip along His timeline. Today is only a mist and will be gone before I notice. He had been leading me right here all along.

Three years ago I heard God ask me to start a blog. "Be vulnerable" He said. I agreed naively, and the blog was born. Shortly after I began, my world felt like it started to fall apart, but actually, it was falling into place. I continued to be transparent as I had promised. Because of my obedience, I ended up chronicling the most amazing time in my life. Since then my Father has guided and directed my steps as I have been willing to venture onto the path that He has for me.

When I am eager to do what He says is best for me even though it is scary, He advances me to the next step. I dare not take one without Him. Since then He has declared that my son and I start a publishing company and that I write this book in a fresh new way but that it be derived from those original blog posts so many years ago. One step leads to another until before I knew it, I had settled into the plans God has for my life.

My life is a reflection of His story. I get to share a bit of how amazing He is every time that I write. I am incredibly grateful for readers who want to hear about my God's heart and how He loves us.

I have found that God has always gone before me and is eagerly waiting for me to join Him. Remember every moment is a chance to do a new thing!

These journal pages are reserved just for you! This is a safe place for you to consider your thoughts and feelings. You can fill them in however you want to. Feel free to disagree with me, but be willing to write down what you think. Each of us needs to look at what we truly believe and to see where it may have come from. Take a few moments just for you and consider what it is that you believe.

Do you think you need a positive life change?

_____

_____

_____

_____

_____

_____

_____

_____

_____

_____

_____

_____

_____

_____

 **Do you think you could change the way you live for ninety days? Does that seem like a long time to you?**

_____

_____

_____

_____

_____

_____

_____

_____

If you knew that you would succeed if you persisted would it make a difference?

_____

_____

_____

_____

_____

_____

_____

_____

What is the most important thing that you need to change in your life right now?

_____

_____

_____

_____

_____

_____

_____

Have you tried to make a big change before? What happened? If you failed why do you think you did? If you succeeded why do you think you did?

_____

_____

_____

_____

_____

_____

_____

_____

_____

_____

_____

Do you think "how you think" matters?

_____

_____

_____

_____

_____

_____

_____

If you make a commitment to do something do you typically follow through? If so what helps you to do so? If not why do you think you give up?

_____

_____

_____

_____

_____

_____

_____

_____

_____

_____

_____

Do you think that God might have a good plan as to how you could change?

_____

_____

_____

_____

_____

_____

_____

_____

If someone told you exactly what you needed to do to succeed would you try what they said?

_____

_____

_____

_____

_____

_____

_____

_____

_____

_____

_____

_____

_____

What if the suggestion came from God?
Would you try what He said? If not why?

_____

_____

_____

_____

_____

_____

_____

_____

If so, are you willing to try to hear Him now? If you are, use this empty space in the book. (If not read the next chapter, it's up to you). With a pen in hand and the blank pages before you, Close your eyes. Ask God a question, or tell Him something you feel that you have needed to say to Him. You don't have to say it out loud, but you can if you want to. Now listen. It may take awhile. It may be that you will be reminded of something or see something right away or it may take several days, but if you have spoken to God, He will talk to you.

God speaks in many ways so you must be willing to believe that He can use people, nature, and anything else in your life to talk to you. If you are listening, you will begin to hear Him.

When you do, write down the responses here. Remember that God often speaks in larger chunks of time than we are used to, so be willing to be patient and if you think it is God write it down.

PART TWO

HOW MY HEART WAS CHANGED

I have an incredible story to tell you if I could only figure out where to start. Many years ago I got married and had my daughter. I did not have faith in Jesus at the time. As the years passed the marriage strained to function and eventually, I wanted a divorce.

My daughter and I moved into our own apartment, and I began over again without my husband. I promised myself that I would work diligently at preserving Lauren's relationship with her father. After all, it wasn't her fault that the marriage had ended. I did everything in my power to keep a good relationship with him. It was the hardest thing that I ever did. Over the years it got easier, and both of us remarried. Now Lauren had four parents instead of two, and somehow it worked.

We lived several blocks from each other which

made it easy for Lauren to see both families. We each had other children, and things got complicated. We shared the responsibilities of her care and the extraneous bills for Lauren such as braces and new school clothing. The majority of the time we all got along, but when we did not, it was extremely uncomfortable. Lauren's dad and I had many disagreements and over time Jenn (his new wife) and I would end up on the phone together trying to smooth things out.

complicated. We shared the responsibilities of her care and the extraneous bills for Lauren such as braces and new school clothing. The majority of the time we all got along, but when we did not, it was extremely uncomfortable. Lauren's dad and I had many disagreements and over time Jenn (his new wife) and I would end up on the phone together trying to smooth things out.

From the first day that Jenn became part of my extended family, I went out of my way to let her know that I appreciated Lauren having another woman in her life who loved her. I sent notes, and we had phone conversations where I intentionally made an effort to express my gratitude. I felt that it was the most important thing that I could do for Jenn, for Lauren, and for myself.

Of course, it was difficult, Jenn was much younger than I was. She was beautiful and smart and friend-ly. The world said that I should not like her. The world told me that she was somehow my competi-tion, my enemy. The world was wrong. We were very much alike. We would most definitely have been friends if my ex-husband had not been involved, but he was. Why were the unspoken rules of the world so different from what I felt? Why would I want to dislike the other woman that was helping to raise my daughter? Why would I want to hate someone instead of love them? Jesus was not yet my Lord or my Savior, but this concept of loving others had always been part of my personality.

As the years passed my daughter and I accepted Jesus as our Lord and Savior. I realized that I truly loved everyone in my ex- husband's family. This agape love was genuine and sincere and moved me to tears. One of the first things God told me to do as His daughter was to pray for their family and to love them. I wanted the best for all of them! It was a freeing, peaceful feeling which bubbled up from a place deep within my newly formed heart in Christ. It was awesome! But no one, and I mean no one, understood. The world still thought that I was supposed to hate my ex-husband and his new wife and their children.

I fought like a salmon swimming upstream against the violent currents of the culture around me. I chose time and time again to dismiss thoughts of insecurity, envy, or comparison. I went out of my way to be loving. I offered help in every way that I could if their family ever had a need.

Some years later my family moved from the Church that I had grown up in, to a new Church. Although I was saved and had established a deep relationship with Christ, my first church had left me hungering for more. From the very first service at the new Church, I became certain that I was home. They read through the Bible verse by verse, they had a program in place for discipleship, and they were active in missional living. They had numerous small groups, a fantastic youth group, and a healthy college-aged ministry.

I had a conversation with Jenn one day and she sounded in need of more like I had been. Even though she attended a Church and was very involved, I could tell that something was missing. First my daughter invited her to come to our Church's prayer and praise night. Jenn lived very far away, but this was a Wednesday night service that took place once a month. Jenn came that Wednesday night and everything began to change. She loved it, and the kids loved the activities that were provided for them. My ex-husband worked on Wednesday nights and was not able to attend. After awhile, I suggested that the family come one Sunday morning a month also. There are four kids at their house, and they live 45 minutes from the Church so I knew that it would be a challenge, but I also knew that they were supposed to be at that Church.

They began coming, and it wasn't too long before they came every Sunday! Lauren, for the first time in her life, had a place where her entire family came together once a week. It was wonderful. I paid careful attention to not make anything awkward for my ex-husband and over time everyone settled into the new Church family.

Little did I know that God had only just started to heal our families. Jenn had gone to Church her whole life, but never honestly given everything to Jesus. One day God spoke to me clearly a word that He wanted me to share with her. Immediately I called her, but she didn't answer. I knew in my spirit that these were the words that He wanted me to say to her and He had given me an urgency about sharing them. How was I going to do this? It was definitely going to be weird, there were so many things that could go wrong... but the urgency that I felt was so intense I knew I had to say it.

The following Sunday, God had it all planned, Jenn had to come to Church alone for some reason that I cannot remember. She sat with us at Church. She sat right next to me. During the middle of worship, when my mind and heart were focused entirely on God, while my hands were raised in adoration and my spirit was praising the Lord, he told me "Say it now." I jumped back a bit startled and looked around..."Do it now, say it now, tell her, tell her, tell her." God said. I leaned over and touched Jenn's shoulder and whispered God's words into her ear. I felt immediate relief and began again to praise God not knowing the implications of what I had just done.

Jenn processed the words on her long ride home alone. I began to wonder if I had just ruined a good thing and made our relationship "weird." I called her and tried to explain that the words were not mine... that they were from the Lord."

Jenn interrupted me. "That's what I needed to hear," she said. And we went on to talk for hours on the phone.

I eventually asked Jenn if I could disciple her (another prompting of the Holy Spirit) and to my delight, she said yes. Since that time we have entered into that deep and sacred relationship, and many amazing things have happened. Jenn got baptized, so did my ex-husband and their children.

Jenn and I have come to love each other as sisters. We are a family. It is amazing! People who see us talking and laughing and hugging each other have no idea who we are to each other. And when they find out they are always floored. God had not only restored us, but He had made us family. Amazing.

God is bigger than broken families! God is bigger than any lack you can mention. God can make a way where there is no way. Listen to me, God can do it and will do it if you will only get out of the way and let Him use you. God can do anything with a yielded and contrite heart. He says love your enemies, and when you do, lives will be changed forever, and God will be glorified.

Jenn and I even went on a mission trip together with my daughter to Africa. To this day we sincerely love each other. As a matter of fact, God has us doing a project together. We are writing a book about what God has done! We both feel that this testimony of ours is meant to be shared together because our story has already ministered to so many. My church filmed a short video about this part of my testimony which was shared with many people. Broken and hurt men and women approached me for months after learning to love the "difficult" people in their lives. I told Jenn that I had a vision of both of us with microphones speaking before crowds of people about our lives. I told her that this would become a ministry some-day.

Writing this book together is the first step to fulfilling that vision. I had attempted to start writing a book about this many times before on my own, but it always felt one-sided. I desired to bring glory to God, and for that to happen, I think that the complete story needs to be told. I asked Jenn to join me and for us to recount the work that the Lord had done in our lives as a team. We genui-nely believe after much prayer that this book will become the forum from which to minister to many broken families. I think that we will have a platform one day to share our story.

Of all of the people that I have ever mentored, this relationship had been more profound than them all. God, after all, is good. Prayer, after all, changes hearts. God's command to pray for their family had produced an abundant, harvest that continues to grow fruit!

Mark chapter four verse twenty says that the seed that fell on good soil represents those who hear and accept God's word and that it will produce a harvest of thirty, sixty, or even a hundred times as much as was originally planted!

My greatest desire is to be good soil. I am so thankful for the opportunity that He gave me to have this as part of my testimony. I love sharing this story of healing, redemption, and love. I choose to love in all circumstances because God promises that it will produce eternal fruit. And it has!

If you are reading this and you also believe in the power of prayer, would you please be praying for Jenn and I as we work on writing our book together. Pray that every word would glorify God and would minister to deeply wounded people. Pray that we will remain faithful to continue writing and meeting together to finish quickly. Pray for the speaking ministry that God has shown us in our future.

My heart wants to obey just as I did when I initially prayed for my ex-husband and his family because out of obedience God will produce amazing things for His kingdom.

These journal pages are reserved just for you!
This is a safe place for you to consider your thoughts and feelings. You can fill them in however you want to. Feel free to disagree with me, but be willing to write down what you think. Each of us needs to look at what we truly believe and to see where it may have come from. Take a few moments just for you and consider what it is that you believe.

Is there anyone in your family that is divorced?

_____
_____
_____
_____

**Are you divorced?
If so, was it amicable?**

_____
_____
_____

What do you think divorce does to a family?

_____

_____

_____

_____

_____

_____

_____

_____

_____

Do you think it is possible for divorced families to reconcile?

_____

_____

_____

_____

_____

_____

_____

_____

_____

 **What do you think you could do to make a place of significant loss in your life any better?**

_____

_____

_____

_____

_____

_____

_____

_____

 **What is a significant loss that you have endured?**

_____

_____

_____

_____

_____

_____

_____

_____

 **How has it affected your life?**

_____
_____
_____
_____
_____
_____
_____
_____
_____

 **Have you learned the ability to forgive others? Have you ever needed to be forgiven?**

_____
_____
_____
_____
_____
_____
_____
_____

Do you think that forgiveness lets the offender off the hook? Do you need to forgive God for something? Do you think that God forgives?

 Do you think that it is possible to forgive and not forget? What things do you think you can do to find a way to forgive someone who has hurt you? Are you willing to try? Would you be willing to ask God what He thinks about your situation?

_____

_____

_____

_____

_____

_____

_____

_____

_____

_____

_____

_____

_____

_____

_____

_____

_____

If so, are you willing to try to hear Him now? If you are, use this empty space in the book. (If not read the next chapter, it's up to you). With a pen in hand and the blank pages before you, Close your eyes. Ask God a question, or tell Him something you feel that you have needed to say to Him. You don't have to say it out loud, but you can if you want to. Now listen. It may take awhile. It may be that you will be reminded of something or see something right away or it may take several days, but if you have spoken to God, He will talk to you.

God speaks in many ways so you must be willing to believe that He can use people, nature, and anything else in your life to talk to you. If you are listening, you will begin to hear Him.

When you do, write down the responses here. Remember that God often speaks in larger chunks of time than we are used to, so be
willing to be patient and if you think it is God write it down.

PART THREE

WHAT LOOKED LIKE THE WRONG DIRECTION

I don't know about you, but we are having a frigid and snowy winter this year. I didn't mind the snow when I had a pick up truck. It was easy; get in, defrost, put the truck in four wheel drive, and go. No shoveling, no worrying. Those were the days. But I no longer have it. I currently have a small economy car which is excellent on gas mileage but horrible in the snow. These days I have to work my day around the time that it will take to shovel my car out. When I decide to go out in a storm, I worry about getting stuck on a hill or careening into a snow drift.

Snow is beautiful. There is nothing more gorgeous than seeing the landscape unified under a blanket of dazzling white. It takes my breath away. But I have learned over the years to dislike the unpredictability and labor that snow often brings.

Currently, it is minus fifteen degrees fahrenheit with the windchill factor, but clear for the moment. We have another storm expected later this week. I think about how quickly the weather changes. Yesterday it was fifty degrees and raining in the morning. It was forty degrees and snowing in the afternoon, and it was fourteen degrees with no precipitation by midnight.

When God first created the earth, the weather was perfect. The Bible says that Adam and Eve walked in the cool of the afternoon with God. It must have been lovely! There was no rain. The earth was originally watered from springs below the surface. Indeed it was paradise.

So many changes came after the fall. Suddenly there was death and disease, and even creation became twisted and broken. Over the years people degraded to the point that God sent a flood of rain from the sky that covered the earth. These days we deal with tornadoes, hurricanes, earthquakes, tsunamis, and snowstorms. All of the creation moans and we moan along with it, waiting impatiently for the day of restoration.

Until then we find ourselves intermingled; life with death, sheep with goats, weeds with flowers. Some walk in health and abundance while others pass away weak and cancerous in their beds. This is not the world that God had intended for us. This world is a result of our sin. People who don't know Jesus as their Lord and Savior don't understand that what He made was good. They twist everything around and blame the God who created the universe. Or worse yet, they don't believe that He exists at all. They point fingers every time that someone they love passes away, every time that a hurricane leaves destruction in its wake, every time that things do not move in perfect order.

Now the strange thing is that all of these thoughts above had been my thoughts yesterday as I sat at the bank drive-through waiting for the teller to come to the window. I had been wondering, pontificating, babbling to myself in my mind. I really didn't have an agenda or a goal, or a point. Just a stream of consciousness. And then it happened. Out of the corner of my eye, I saw something.

You see, where my car was, I could look up past a slight incline to a major road. The speed limit there is forty five miles per hour, and the traffic was heavy. Something caught my attention and quickly halted my thoughts. A snow plow was backing up in full-on traffic. I watched in disbelief as cars swerved to get around him. He was moving slowly and steadily backward along the right-hand side of the road. His plow was raised in the air, and I could hear a faint back up signal beeping into the cold air. "Oh my goodness" I actually said out loud, "What is he doing?! He is going to get hit!" I watched intently as we all tend to watch potential accidents, with my eyes glued to the truck.

Somehow he maneuvered backward without hitting any cars. Honestly, he was so big and heavy that he probably would have totaled whatever he ran into. When the truck finally came to rest he was almost out of my view. That is when his plow came down. I watched as he lowered it to the ground. Cars were still whizzing by him as he stood there still and silent. He began to plow the snow that had drifted onto the side of the road. It had not been visible from my vantage point, but he had seen it. He pushed and plowed and cleared the way. I watched cars beginning to see what he was doing, and they started to follow him in the now clear lane.

I hadn't noticed that before he plowed all of the cars had become bottlenecked into one lane. If he hadn't come along and dislodged the obstruction things would have gotten even more chaotic. As a matter of fact, it would have been more dangerous to leave the road obstructed than to have driven backward as he did.

As I sat there contemplating what I had just seen it occurred to me that sometimes God goes backward in the midst of on oncoming traffic for us. It feels dangerous. It seems like the wrong way, but what if backward was really the best way to go?

Sometimes we think, "Oh my goodness! What is He doing?!" when God begins to backup to help us dislodge something, not of His kingdom that has drifted onto our path. If He doesn't help us clear it, chaos will ensue, and there will be an obstruction that can keep us from moving forward safely.

I remember hearing God yesterday remind me of words from the book of Luke in chapter nine, "No one who puts his hand to the plow and looks back is fit for the kingdom of God." Now I know that this refers to a plow in a field, not a snowplow. And honestly, I was just as surprised as you are that this is what God had said. I mean He is God,

He was aware of everything that I had been thinking. The analogy didn't seem to jive. Because it didn't make a lot of sense to me, when I went home I read a few of the verses before Luke chapter nine verse sixty two. Verse fifty seven said, "As they were going along the road someone said to him, 'I will follow you wherever you go.' And Jesus said to him, 'Foxes have holes, and birds of the air have nests, but the son of Man has nowhere to lay his head,' To another, he said, 'Follow me.' But he said, 'Lord, let me first go and bury my father.' And Jesus said to him, 'Leave the dead to bury their own dead. But as for you go and proclaim the kingdom of God.' Yet another said, 'I will follow you, Lord, but let me first say farewell to those at my home.' Jesus said to him, 'No one who puts his hand to the plow and looks back is fit for the kingdom of God."

God had interrupted me during an ordinary task; sitting in line at a drive through. He had placed me strategically in a place where I could view the road. He had orchestrated the cars and the snowplow and even the snow drifting onto the street. He wanted me to look up and take note. I believe that God speaks through the everyday occurrences that are all around us. I know that He wants to guide us, teach us, encourage us and love us. I genuinely think that if I hadn't noticed the truck, that God would have spoken to me at another time, in another way.

But it is sad to think of how often we might miss His promptings. He had gotten my attention and then had delivered a Biblical truth that He wanted me to dig further into at this challenging time in my life.

At the time I was newly unemployed by no fault of my own. The woman that I had worked for eight years had just passed away. I, like the cars, had been just going along the road. I have said to God, "I will follow You wherever You go." And here He was reminding me that Jesus said if I were to "follow Him" I may have nowhere to stop, and rest...it was not going to be comfortable or easy. I would not have security. Jesus has asked me to Follow him, and I must remember that this means that I can't put anything else before Him, not even things that the world tells me are necessary and even good. Instead, He beckons me to go and proclaim the kingdom of God. I must be willing to live my life as He directs me, this life that is no longer my own.

God reminded me that there are no exceptions. That if I choose to follow Him I cannot look back. He expects me to move forward. He tells me that He is making a way for me even if it seems like what He is doing is as crazy as driving backward in heavy traffic. He is God, and He will do things His way. He can see what I cannot see from my vantage point just as the snowplow driver could see the snow that had drifted onto the road when I couldn't.

What He was doing made no sense to me until I could see that snow on the plow as He was clearing the way.

God might look like He is driving backward. My situation might seem out of control or crazy, but I know His character, and I know that whatever He is doing is for my good.

God is making a way for me where there was no way, and at the very same moment with the very same gesture, He is also reminding me that I cannot look back or give in to the world around me. No matter what seems right or sensible, I must look forward and plow ahead following only Him.

These journal pages are reserved just for you! This is a safe place for you to consider your thoughts and feelings. You can fill them in however you want to. Feel free to disagree with me, but be willing to write down what you think. Each of us needs to look at what we truly believe and to see where it may have come from. Take a few moments just for you and consider what it is that you believe.

Do you ever notice things around you that seem out of place?

Do you ever wonder why you see them?

_____
_____
_____
_____
_____
_____
_____
_____
_____

Have you ever been the only one to see a situation from a different perspective?

_____
_____
_____
_____
_____
_____
_____
_____
_____
_____

Why do you think you notice things happening around you?

_____

_____

_____

_____

_____

_____

_____

_____

_____

Do you think everyday moments can speak wisdom into your life?

_____

_____

_____

_____

_____

_____

_____

_____

_____

Where do you think that wisdom comes from?

_____

_____

_____

_____

_____

_____

_____

_____

_____

When You encounter an eye opening truth, do you let it change the course of your life?

_____

_____

_____

_____

_____

_____

_____

_____

Do you think God is wise?

_____

_____

_____

_____

_____

_____

_____

_____

If you believe God has wisdom would you be willing to listen to Him?

_____

_____

_____

_____

_____

_____

_____

_____

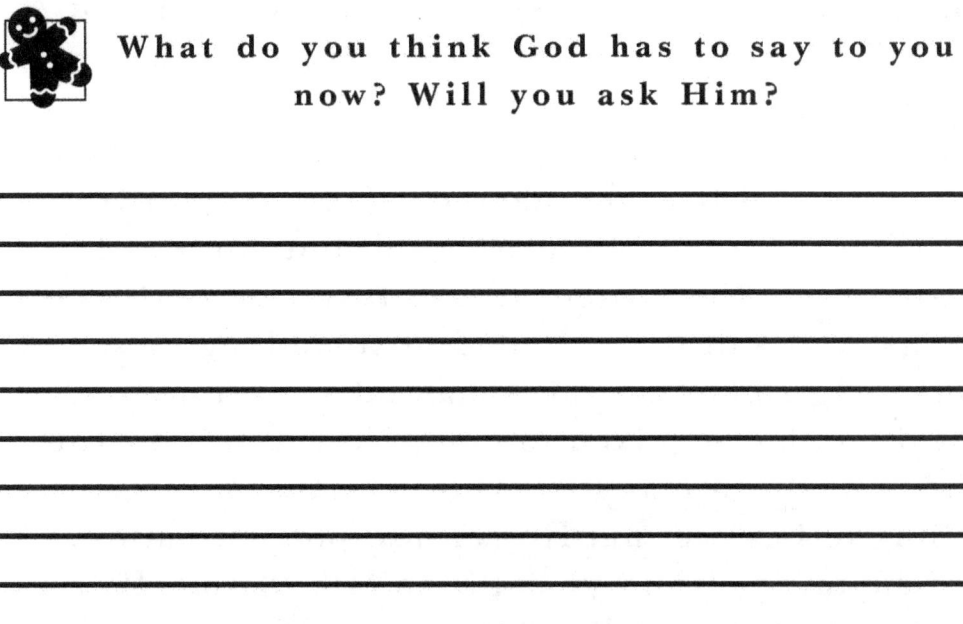

What do you think God has to say to you now? Will you ask Him?

If so, are you willing to try to hear Him now? If you are, use this empty space in the book. (If not read the next chapter, it's up to you). With a pen in hand and the blank pages before you, Close your eyes. Ask God a question, or tell Him something you feel that you have needed to say to Him. You don't have to say it out loud, but you can if you want to. Now listen. It may take awhile. It may be that you will be reminded of something or see something right away or it may take several days, but if you have spoken to God, He will talk to you.

God speaks in many ways so you must be willing to believe that He can use people, nature, and anything else in your life to talk to you. If you are listening, you will begin to hear Him.

When you do, write down the responses here. Remember that God often speaks in larger chunks of time than we are used to, so be
willing to be patient and if you think it is God write it down.

PART FOUR

HE BRINGS THE DEAD TO LIFE

I worked as a private duty aide with a 93-year-old woman named Patty. I had been with her for eight years. From the beginning, it was clear that God had given me another long-term assignment. I had been with the couple that I had worked for previously for eight and a half years. This kind of longevity in the elder care field is unheard of. Most clients are with you for a year or less by the time that they need private duty. But when God has a plan, anything is possible.

With my previous patients Jon and Evelyn, God used me not only to care for them, but He allowed me to be integral in bringing Jon to Christ! Jon was ninety years old at the time. It took years of his seeing my life, which I had turned over to God, for him to be open to my speaking about Jesus. It took layer upon layer of love and relationship to advance to the place where he was able to accept

Jesus as his Lord and Savior. At the time I marveled at God reaching the "unreachable." Jon was a wealthy man who had everything that he needed until his wife Evelyn suffered a series of strokes that took her short-term memory from her and stole his dreams from him. Jon ran the household when I first arrived. But as the years ticked by, Jon began to get sick until one day he was diagnosed with cancer. Everything began to change as this man who thought that he was in "control" began to realize that he could choose very little of what was happening in his life. Jon became bedridden and began to open up to the possibility that he had missed what life was truly all about.

One night his nurse, a Christian woman who had been ministering to Jon along with me, called. It was three o'clock in the morning. "Amanda, Jon is having nightmares, and he is terrified. I don't know what to say to him and when I prayed God said to call you. "I am sorry it's so late,", she said barely taking a breath. I could hear the concern in her voice. "No problem," I said not having a clue what I could do to help him. She put Jon on the phone. I threw up a quick prayer asking God for an inroad to present the gospel one more time. You see, Jon had been "over-churched" growing up.

He had been forced to go against his will and as soon as he was old enough, stopped going altogether. Jon never thought that Jesus was something he needed, until now. Everything was going so differently from what he had planned. His money had allowed him to book private sailing trips in exotic places for most of his adult life. He had aspired to retire on a tropical island, and now here he was trapped in his bed. Stuck inside his beautiful home for the rest of his life.

"I am scared," He said matter-of-factly. "I don't know what to do anymore," he said. "Jon do you want to pray?" I asked as I always did. "Yes," he answered sheepishly. We prayed, and he explained his nightmare to me. When we were done, I felt prompted to ask him if he wanted to receive Christ. Over the years I must have asked him thirty times. Every time I asked, he would smile warmly and say, 'I don't think so dear but thank you for asking, I'm okay." This time he said yes! I was sitting there all alone in my dark living room in the middle of the night. This is not how I thought it would happen if it ever did. I began telling him that he should repeat after me as I prayed, but only if it was what he really felt in his heart. He agreed. When we got to the part about his being "a sinner" I thought for sure that he would stop, but to my delight, he kept on going! When we were through, I got the blessing of hearing him lift up his first prayer to God. He thanked Him, and he apologized for his life. It was simple, raw and beautiful.

Now here I am eight years into my journey with Patty. Time seems to have flown by. Patty had a major stroke and had gone into a retirement home. I had known somehow from my first day with her that this pairing was going to be just as unique as it was with Jon and Evelyn. God had assured me that there was much to learn.

And at the age of ninety two, Patty also accepted Jesus as her Lord and Savior. I couldn't believe it! Older hearts get crusty and hard sometimes. Years of head knowledge and selfish habits build impenetrable walls around a soul. But God can do anything. God wants to receive everyone as a son and a daughter. He sent Jesus to save the world. He wants noone to be lost. I was beginning to realize that God had sent me to help them, and also to teach me tenacity. One day when I went into work, one of the staff nurses told me that Patty had had a rough weekend. She had what is called "syncope" which is a heart event.

The heart actually stops. She had experienced two episodes over the weekend, one on Saturday and one on Sunday. Patty seemed weak and tired when I arrived that day, but still very much her stubborn and witty self. We made it through the morning just fine. When it was time for me to go, I set about putting things in order and making sure that Patty had everything that she needed. As I was leaving, she looked up at me and told me that she needed to go to the bathroom.

Patty had an oxygen mask on and a blanket over her lap and a long thick robe wrapped around her. She needed help, and honestly, I didn't trust the nurses to get to her there on time, so I put down my pocketbook and book bag and went over to her chair to help her up. "Let me help you," I said.

I got her up and held her arm as she maneuvered her walker through the tiny room. She was weak and unsteady. After she was done, we turned to leave the bathroom.

I was still walking with my arms linked up under hers so she would not fall. Suddenly she began to lean drastically to the left. This is a sign of a stroke. I pulled her into an upright position and moved behind her with both of my arms looped up under hers, and we walked together towards her chair. We were only a foot from our goal when I felt her legs begin to shake. I braced myself for the weight of her body.

Almost as soon as I did her body slumped, and I was holding her dead weight. I tried to turn to get her to the chair, but she was just too heavy. I lowered her gently to the floor still keeping my arms under hers to keep her in a sitting position. I dragged her to the call bell for the nurses and pushed the button. She began to gasp, and then she exhaled, and there was no breath at all. I looked down at her chest, and it was not moving. I reached to her arm and grabbed her wrist and felt for a pulse. There was none. I was already going through so much in my life, was Patty really going to die in my arms today?

The time that passed seemed like hours. I would guess it was only thirty seconds. No breath. No heartbeat. Nothing. I prayed. "God thank you for allowing me to be here." Out of instinct as I waited for the nurses, I touched Patty's arm and rubbed my hand back and forth. "Come on sweetie. Come

on Patty hang in there it's Amanda, I am with you."
I don't know what I was thinking. She had coded. I
think maybe it was just that instinct to care for
people that I have. Suddenly the arm that I was
rubbing moved a little. I rubbed and patted and
called her name sweetly. The next thing I knew her
hand was moving and her fingers wiggled and she
began to breathe again. The nurses finally arrived
and helped her into her chair. They started to take
her vitals, and I stepped back and watched them
work on her.

Jon had been dead spiritually, and God had
brought him to life just before he passed away
from cancer. God has blessed me to see many go
from death to life over the years. I have been in a
lot of hospice situations with people during the
sacred time of dying. But this was the first time
that I held someone in my arms who had stopped
breathing. The first time that a heart stopped
beating. Patty's body was resurrected somehow. We
may never fully understand the intricacies of the
human body. God makes amazing things.

Those 16 years had been a training ground for
me. God put me in jobs that allowed me to be
home to care for my children as they grew up and
He had taught me how to love stubborn, crusty,
hardened hearts patiently. God showed me first
hand that nothing is impossible for Him. Even what
looks as if it is dead, has a life at His command.

I find myself encouraged today thinking about
how God is always doing a new thing. I look
outside at the stark winter branches. They look so

grey and lifeless and yet inside, where I cannot see, God is working His mystery, and they will again spring forth in green splendor. The season will come when everything is resurrected and in bloom. Although I am in a difficult season... this too will pass. What looks dead can come to life in God's kingdom by his Holy Spirit power. He is always making things new.

I am reminded that I cannot see what He is doing, but I can always trust in who He is. He has never let me down. He won't start now.

Holding a life that had departed even if for a moment and then seeing the breath enter it again has left me different somehow. My God is able to give and take away life! He is loving and kind and merciful, not wanting any to perish. He begs us to consider that He is doing a new thing. He asks us to perceive it. He promises to make a way for us.

These journal pages are reserved just for you! This is a safe place for you to consider your thoughts and feelings. You can fill them in however you want to. Feel free to disagree with me, but be willing to write down what you think. Each of us needs to look at what we truly believe and to see where it may have come from. Take a few moments just for you and consider what it is that you believe.

Have you ever had a job helping others?

_____

_____

_____

_____

_____

_____

_____

_____

_____

_____

_____

_____

_____

If not, have any of your jobs provided you opportunities to have a positive influence in other people's lives?

_____

_____

_____

_____

_____

_____

_____

_____

_____

What did you do with those opportunities? Did you take them? What was the result?

_____

_____

_____

_____

_____

_____

_____

_____

_____

How has the death of people you love effected you?

_____

_____

_____

_____

_____

_____

_____

_____

_____

_____

Are you afraid of dying?

_____

_____

_____

_____

_____

_____

_____

_____

_____

_____

What do you believe happens to you when you die? Why is that what you believe?

_____

_____

_____

_____

_____

_____

_____

_____

_____

_____

Why do you think people die?

_____

_____

_____

_____

_____

_____

_____

_____

_____

_____

How would you define Heaven?

_____

_____

_____

_____

_____

_____

_____

_____

Do you think everyone goes to Heaven? If so why do you think so?

_____

_____

_____

_____

_____

_____

_____

_____

Do you think God can revive things that you thought were dead in your life?

_____

_____

_____

_____

_____

_____

_____

_____

_____

Do you know what the bible says about the afterlife? Do you want to know?

_____

_____

_____

_____

_____

_____

_____

_____

_____

What do you think God has to say to you about death? Will you ask Him?

If so, are you willing to try to hear Him now? If you are, use this empty space in the book. (If not read the next chapter, it's up to you). With a pen in hand and the blank pages before you, Close your eyes. Ask God a question, or tell Him something you feel that you have needed to say to Him. You don't have to say it out loud, but you can if you want to. Now listen. It may take awhile. It may be that you will be reminded of something or see something right away or it may take several days, but if you have spoken to God, He will talk to you.

God speaks in many ways so you must be willing to believe that He can use people, nature, and anything else in your life to talk to you. If you are listening, you will begin to hear Him.

When you do, write down the responses here. Remember that God often speaks in larger chunks of time than we are used to, so be willing to be patient and if you think it is God write it down.

PART FIVE

MORNINGS WITH MAMA

I have some beautiful memories of my childhood. I also have not so wonderful memories. Through the years I have changed so much. Most of my painful memories have been transformed into lessons learned. They were proficient teachers. I have determined to let go of what cannot be changed and more importantly to hold onto the things that can be. I have become who I was meant to be, it may have taken me more than half of a century to get here, but I have arrived at a place where I enjoy my life to its fullest every day.

You see, I have come to realize that I am not the only one who has changed and at the core of that realization is the essence of truly loving others. I used to think that love meant so many different things than what I now know. I had been reared on fairy tales that were never going to come true. I had believed so many lies about who I was that I

Although our family professed to be Christian and went faithfully to a church building every Sunday morning, I had never met Jesus. I lived in a home where we prayed the same prayer each evening before bed and another before every meal. I never saw a Bible being read except for the fleeting moments I watched everyone struggle to find their place in the dusty old Bibles lying along the church pews.

As a child church didn't resonate with me. It made no sense. There was no joy, no healing, no love. We entered a building wrought with rules of how we must dress and behave. The faces of all of the people around me looked stern and stiff. No one seemed to like being there and the man who climbed steadily to the top of the lofty pulpit was shrouded in a black robe that looked like fantastic bat wings when he raised his arms during his fiery speeches about things a child just cannot comprehend.

Alas, the Sunday school classes where not any better and most weeks I begged to sit in the pew with my parents. Their regular seat at the time was up in the balcony. At least that way I was able to look down on the scary man in the black robe. From there he looked little and much less frightening.

Trauma had affected my life. At that time, the events which traumatized me were unknown to my parents. I was left anxious and depressed, and by the ripe old age of five, I had daily migraine headaches which often sent me to lay on my bed in the darkness with a cold, wet washcloth over my eyes. Not the carefree childhood that I would like to recall. I would not share the full details of my traumatic experiences with them until I was well into my forties, but all of the poor decisions that I would make from that point on would pile sharply onto this faulty foundation.

I was an intelligent child who loved to write and to tell stories from cardboard cut out stages. One of my fondest memories is how my mother would put down whatever she was doing to watch me perform or to read my latest short story. To be fair my father did as well, but this story is about my mom and I so I will share about dad another time.

After living many years in rebellion to my parents and to God, one day I gave my life to Jesus. As soon as I did, He immediately began tearing down the walls that had been keeping me prisoner for the majority of my life. He crashed through and destroyed the strongholds of the enemy, He began to pour a perfect foundation in my heart. On it, He built the most beautiful life for me to live.

As Jesus worked in me, I came alive. I became a new person, the person I had actually been made to be. And, as I grew and my life unfolded exposing this beauty placed in me by God, I was able to let go of unforgiveness and extend grace just as I had received it from God.

During my rebellious years, my mom and dad prayed for me. But to be honest, they never really believed that God could get ahold of my heart. One day, He did, and everything about me changed in an instant. I bought a study Bible and started to wake up at five a.m. each morning to pray out loud and to read God's word. I couldn't get enough of Him. I sat for hours reading and journaling and asking questions. Patiently and lovingly God provided me the answers. My eyes and ears were opened to spiritual things, and my world took on a whole new dimension.

During these years, my mom saw the life of Jesus in me and wanted more for herself. She began to ask me questions and to study the Bible. We talked about who God is and our relationships with Him. She caught the same enthusiasm for His kingdom that I had, and it was just beautiful to watch.

Somewhere along the way I looked around and realized that my mama was in her eighties. How long would we have these fantastic conversations together? For how many days or months or years could we settle in and learn from each other? How long would we connect in this deep way that other people just couldn't understand?

The connection of our agreement in the wonder of who God is and what He has done in our lives had opened up a deeper channel for everything in our relationship. We were more patient and kind and silly and well, just more, more, more...

I didn't want to miss a thing. I felt that I had wasted so many years of my life already. So one day I decided that I was going to talk to my mom on the phone every morning before I started my day. Looking back I can't remember when this started, but not a day goes by that I don't speak with her. Some days we pray together. Some days we laugh (a lot). Some days we don't talk for as long. Some days I am late for work because our conversation is that good that I can't stop it.

I began to call this particular time, "Mornings with Mama." I always wanted to write about it. This is just a start. Thanks to my daily journaling habit (something I have done since I was little), one day this will become a book. Its pages will overflow with love and wisdom. There will be laughter and tears in those pages too. And one day, a day I hate to think of, I will not be able to talk with Mom anymore. One day she will go to be with Jesus, but He is the one who gave her to me in the first place. What better place for her to go?

Until that day arrives, I will take the time to cherish this special relationship with her and the pivotal moments from it that have directed the paths of our lives since we began making the time to be together every day.

These journal pages are reserved just for you! This is a safe place for you to consider your thoughts and feelings. You can fill them in however you want to. Feel free to disagree with me, but be willing to write down what you think. Each of us needs to look at what we truly believe and to see where it may have come from. Take a few moments just for you and consider what it is that you believe.

How do you remember your childhood?

_____

_____

_____

_____

_____

_____

_____

_____

_____

_____

_____

_____

How are you different now?

_____
_____
_____
_____
_____
_____
_____
_____
_____

Has your family changed over the years?

_____
_____
_____
_____
_____
_____
_____
_____
_____

What did you grow up believing?

_____

_____

_____

_____

_____

_____

_____

_____

_____

Did you go through a rebellious period?

_____

_____

_____

_____

_____

_____

_____

_____

_____

Has your life influenced anyone else in your family?

_____

_____

_____

_____

_____

_____

_____

_____

_____

How have those changes affected your relationship?

_____

_____

_____

_____

_____

_____

_____

_____

_____

What efforts can you make to make a relationship with someone in your family better?

_____

_____

_____

_____

_____

_____

_____

_____

_____

Can you start some new positive traditions?

_____

_____

_____

_____

_____

_____

_____

_____

_____

What would those new traditions look like?

_____

_____

_____

_____

_____

_____

_____

_____

Do you think God can actually talk to you? Do you think God cares about your family?

_____

_____

_____

_____

_____

_____

_____

_____

_____

Have you ever tried to hear God? What do you think God has to say about your family?

_____
_____
_____
_____
_____
_____
_____
_____
_____
_____

If so, are you willing to try to hear Him now? If you are, use this empty space in the book. (If not read the next chapter, it's up to you). With a pen in hand and the blank pages before you, Close your eyes. Ask God a question, or tell Him something you feel that you have needed to say to Him. You don't have to say it out loud, but you can if you want to. Now listen. It may take awhile. It may be that you will be reminded of something or see something right away or it may take several days, but if you have spoken to God, He will talk to you.

God speaks in many ways so you must be willing to believe that He can use people, nature, and anything else in your life to talk to you. If you are listening, you will begin to hear Him.

When you do, write down the responses here. Remember that God often speaks in larger chunks of time than we are used to, so be willing to be patient and if you think it is God write it down.

_____

_____

_____

_____

_____

_____

_____

PART SIX

EIGHT
THOUSAND PROMISES

If you got on a plane and brought your luggage, you would expect to go to the luggage carousel to claim it when you land, right? Well God sends us out to new destinations and into new situations every day. There are loads of promises that we are meant to carry with us. When we arrive at each destination, God's next step for us is to go and claim these promises. There are over eight thousand promises in God's word. Most aren't placed in our hands, but they are set within our reach. Just as when we claim our luggage at the airport if we are to receive God's promises, we must know a few things. First, we need to know where to go to claim them. Second, we must understand the promises well enough to recognize them when we see them. And third, we need to be willing to go over to them and pick them up to carry them away.

Can you imagine the luggage claim of God's promises? There would be heavy bags of love, redemption, and power slowly turning before you. Suitcases that scream out, "chosen, victorious, holy, worthy, righteous" in neon bright colors whizzing by. All of them on the turn style of truths that God created for you to pick up and claim as your own. All of them are freely given. All of them have your name on them.

In the book of Joshua, God promises to give us every place we actually put our feet. It means that we have to get up and go somewhere if we want to receive something. Perhaps we desire a new job, a new relationship, any new beginning. We can't just sit comfortably at home and expect to receive anything more than we already have. In this current age, we can order just about anything we want online and get it the same day. It's hard for us to remember that we need to step outside of our comfort zones to receive the promises that we have not yet claimed as our own. We have to get up and go somewhere that may be uncomfortable and uncertain, but in the going there is purpose and there is life! Real life, not a virtual social media cyber life. We have allowed ourselves convenience in every area of existence, and I believe we have robbed an entire generation of the joy of effort, of the feeling of satisfaction that a physical accomplishment can bring to a situation.

Before you can claim what is yours, you have to know what God says is yours. How familiar are you with God's promises? And of those promises that you know, do you believe that these things are really for you? God expects us to believe Him and

He expects us to take action based on that belief. Even if you have never read the Bible, the promises God has are for you too. If we dare to believe that He is who He says He is. We must find a way to understand who we are in relation to Him. He wants to have a relationship with us. We would need to put away any preconceived notions about Him and start fresh.

It amazes me how many people refer to themselves as "spiritual" but don't believe in God or in Jesus. Many people look at the created but do not see the Creator. That decision is up to each individual, but I want you to know there is a free coupon book of good things for your life just sitting there waiting for you. You don't even need to own a Bible these days to read one, all you need to do is look some things up online if you want to see what I am talking about. What if you were willing to check out whatever need you have right now out in this way. How about, instead of looking up the best place to eat dinner tonight, you looked to see what God had to say about anxiety, health or financial stability? Whatever you are going through, the Bible offers wisdom that the world cannot. I am not saying that the Bible is a resource to be used exclusively for what you need at the moment, but it is a place to start.

Too often I hear of someone going through difficult times, even those who pray, pleading from their living room sofa asking God to step in for them, but they aren't willing to do anything. What I have found in my own tough times, is to ask God for His help and to thank Him for who He is. These are fantastic things to do in times of trouble, but next comes listening for His answer. And when He does you must get up and go do whatever He has instructed.

Do you think God can talk to you? I know most of my life I would have called you crazy if you said yes. But over time I have learned to hear Him. He doesn't typically speak to us audibly, although He can. God speaks in everyday moments. Through the things that He has made. God speaks through people in your life. He talks however the heck He wants to! I think I used to limit Him by needing to be sure I had actually heard Him.

I started to journal daily, and as I did, I found that God speaks in large chunks of time sometimes telling me the same thing in many ways. Because my brain and busy schedule only allow me to retain one day at a time, I often miss what He has been showing me. By journaling, I can go back and look over a week, a month, or even a year and see from a new perspective the explicit messages He has been conveying. Some people want to call these something else, but I challenge you to be open to it actually being God. And if it is Him what else does He have to say?

If He really did make everything and really does love you, could your life become more peaceful, powerful and fruitful? Would you find a way to receive real rest and not waste your energy on good plans, but instead walk in amazing adventures? That is what happened to me! I was beyond skeptical, I made fun of God and Christians and the Bible and Church. At one point I thought myself so intelligent that there couldn't possibly be a God and if there was, I had declared

He was distant, unfair, and cold. He never gave up
on believing in me though. He loved me
unconditionally and eventually during the most
painful time of my life, His voice became louder
than my own.

All throughout the Bible, God gives battle plans
to people who want to hear His instructions. Even
when God's plan might be that He is the one that
will do the fighting for you, He still requires you to
get up and to stand. Nowhere does God say in the
bible to just pray or to only hope. As a matter of
fact, when God does the fighting, He does so
differently than we would. We must remember that
God's ways are not our ways. His thoughts are
higher than our thoughts. He thinks differently
than we think.

Let's take a quick look at the battle of Jericho.
This was a war fought by people who were walking
in the desert against a massive city with a thick
stone wall all around it. God fought this battle for
His people, but He did it His way, and He required
them to follow some very particular instructions.
To adhere to these plans meant that they must have
heard God speak. To have heard God speak meant
that they must have listened to what He said
because frankly, these instructions sounded ludi-
crous.

God told them to get up and go to the city of
Jericho. He instructed them to travel around the
giant stone wall that surrounded the town filled
with armed people every day for 7 days. On the
seventh day, they were to sound a trumpet, and
along with that trumpet sound they all had to shout
as loud as they could. God promised if they did,

the walls would come falling down. God didn't say, "Stay here and watch Me knock the wall down," He said "Come with Me, and we will all do it together. Follow my instructions and then claim the victory that I have promised you!"

I know some of you are saying, but what about the times when God did the fighting?" You are right, there are many stories where God confused the enemy or tricked the enemy, and His people didn't need to do much. In the book of Judges, there was a man named Gideon. He ended up with only three hundred men to fight against a huge army. They listened for God's instruction. God's plan for them was to surround the enemy at night each with a lit torch under a clay pot. They stood at the top of the hill, each with their bright light hidden, until their trumpets sounded and they smashed their clay jars. They each held a trumpet and a light and shouted all together, "A sword for the Lord and for Gideon." Every man stood in his place around the camp, and all of the armies below ran. The enemy cried out and fled. When they blew the three hundred trumpets, the Lord set every man's sword below them against their comrades. The enemy fled far away.

In Exodus, Moses tells the people not to fear and to stand firm. He said that the Lord would save them and that the Egyptians they were running from would never be seen again. The Lord would fight for them if they would only be silent and stand up. The people only had to stand up, stay in position silently and watch God. God could have answered their prayers by just wiping out all of the Egyptians while they were still in Egypt. God was teaching His people to ask, to listen, to get up, and then to obey His instructions. God always gives us a role to play in the deliverance that He grants us.

When you find yourself in that place where you need help, what if you tried asking God? What if you said something like: "God, what exactly is it that You want me to do? These are my problems, and I will wait for your directions. I am sitting here, listening for You. I am waiting on Your battle plan. When you tell me what You want me to do, I promise to stand up, and go and do it!"

So much victory is ours to claim thanks to what Jesus did on the cross for us. When we ask God for directions, and we get up and go follow them we are transformed. We are no longer who we used to be. When we do things God's way, we build stronger muscles, and we achieve greater faith. God strengthens us in the trials that He allows. He changes our name and He transforms us. We are incapable of doing what God has for us to do on our own, but in obedience to Him, and the plan of action that He has for us, all things are possible. God, wants us to lean on Him. Are you willing to try?

These journal pages are reserved just for you! This is a safe place for you to consider your thoughts and feelings. You can fill them in however you want to. Feel free to disagree with me, but be willing to write down what you think. Each of us needs to look at what we truly believe and to see where it may have come from. Take a few moments just for you and consider what it is that you believe.

What do you expect from life?

_____

_____

_____

_____

_____

_____

_____

_____

_____

_____

_____

_____

_____

_____

How have those expectations let you down? Did they change your view of people or the world?

_____

_____

_____

_____

_____

_____

_____

_____

_____

Do you feel that you deserve certain things that you have never received?

_____

_____

_____

_____

_____

_____

_____

_____

_____

Has anyone ever broken a promise to you?
How did that make you feel?

_____

_____

_____

_____

_____

_____

_____

_____

_____

Has God ever let you down?
If so, then how?

_____

_____

_____

_____

_____

_____

_____

_____

_____

What were your expectations of Him?

_____
_____
_____
_____
_____
_____
_____
_____
_____
_____

Were you following His ways or expecting Him to bless your own?

_____
_____
_____
_____
_____
_____
_____
_____
_____
_____

Do you think it's unfair of God to ask you to live a certain way? If yes or no why?

_____

_____

_____

_____

_____

_____

_____

_____

Are you willing to look at God as a parent, as a Father, and if so, in that context doesn't He need to have some rules for His kids to keep them safe?

_____

_____

_____

_____

_____

_____

_____

As a child did you understand or like your parents rules?

_____
_____
_____
_____
_____
_____
_____
_____
_____

Do you think God can actually talk to you?

_____
_____
_____
_____
_____
_____
_____
_____
_____

Have you ever tried to hear God?

_____

_____

_____

_____

_____

_____

_____

_____

_____

If so, are you willing to try to hear Him now? If you are, use this empty space in the book. (If not read the next chapter, it's up to you). With a pen in hand and the blank pages before you, Close your eyes. Ask God a question, or tell Him something you feel that you have needed to say to Him. You don't have to say it out loud, but you can if you want to. Now listen. It may take awhile. It may be that you will be reminded of something or see something right away or it may take several days, but if you have spoken to God, He will talk to you.

God speaks in many ways so you must be willing to believe that He can use people, nature, and anything else in your life to talk to you. If you are listening, you will begin to hear Him.

When you do, write down the responses here. Remember that God often speaks in larger chunks of time than we are used to, so be willing to be patient and if you think it is God write it down.

PART SEVEN

IN THE VALLEY OF THE DRY BONES

Chapter thirty-seven of the book of Ezekiel in the Old Testament of the Bible is a fantastic story. It is so incredible, really, that I may not have believed it to be possible. Yes, me the born again, fired up, crazy about Jesus lady. Even I don't always understand God. Don't get me wrong, I still want to believe Him, but I have a heart problem that often gets in the way.

I have read this story numerous times. I thought that I knew every detail, but God, as He often does, challenged me to apply this to my own life, to my own heart, to my own skeletons.

This story is the recorded vision of a prophet of God. His name, Ezekiel, means "God Strengthens" in the Hebrew language. He was a prophet who was someone who professed to not only hear directly from God but to speak for God as well. To be a prophet, you could never be wrong. If you didn't hear God correctly, then you were not considered a prophet. As a prophet you needed to be on point one hundred percent of the time! Pretty tough odds for a person, but easy for God.

Ezekiel was among the captives taken to Babylon at the first fall of Jerusalem. He wrote the book of Ezekiel while in captivity. As far as assignments from the Lord go, he sure got a difficult one. Who wants to hear from a God who allows you to live as a captive, right? But the story doesn't go like that. God had given His chosen people many chances to do the right thing. They never did despite all of His warnings that there would be consequences and just like every other parent I know, when His kids didn't listen, God had no choice but to follow through with the punishment He hoped would set them straight.

Even so, God continued to speak and to offer His comfort, His presence, and His love in many ways during those years. Today I want to talk to you about a particular vision that God gave to Ezekiel. This vision would find him in the center of a valley filled with dry bones.

How bizarre. To recap the story for you, Ezekiel says that it was because of God that he was there. He says that the Spirit of God brought him to that place and placed him right in the middle of it. Not at the edge, but directly on top of the piles of bones strewn across the valley floor. He recounts that there were a great many bones, so don't just picture one broken skeleton. These bones were described as very dry.

Think about this for a minute. For piles of extremely dry bones to be on a valley floor, this was most likely the remains of a battle.

Wars were fought in the valleys in that time. Imagine, valiant soldiers each fighting for his life. Each of them having died. Imagine the struggle, the wounds, the bleeding, the pain. These bodies must have sat in the sun decomposing while wild animals came and fed on their flesh. And after time, when there was nothing left to pick from their bones, they lay there exposed to the elements and beginning to dry out. They were brittle and fragile, I would think. Some of them must have snapped underfoot as the weight of this prophet walked over them. As a matter of fact, in the vision, the Lord made Ezekiel walk back and forth over the bones. He could most likely feel them under the worn soles of his leather sandals. Ezekiel could see them with his eyes and hear the sounds that his footsteps made as he made his way over them. I imagine he must have had to stretch his arms out to keep his balance. It must have felt eerie and overwhelming.

In the vision, God asks Ezekiel if the bones can live. The prophet responds with wisdom and says that only the Lord knows for sure. God tells him to speak to the bones and to tell them to "hear the word of the Lord." The Lord tells him to say to the bones that God was going to make breath enter them. He would make tendons and skin come onto them. And that they would come to life. As the prophet followed God's commands and spoke to the bones, he began to hear a rattling sound! Seriously? Wow, the bones started to reconnect back together into skeletons. Next, the prophet spoke to the tendons and the skin. And finally, God told Ezekiel to command the breath of God to enter these bodies standing on the valley floor. I can't even imagine how I would feel at that point, but then the breath entered them, and they were alive! There stood entirely resurrected men. And remember these were soldiers who had died fighting together, now unified by this new life. They were ready to move out from that place. The Scripture actually calls them a vast army.

Seeing this on the big screen with all of the special effects that Hollywood would bring would be nothing less than amazing. A movie that shared something this insane would be a blockbuster hit. Most people have never opened a Bible and never heard this story, so I am honestly surprised that someone hasn't found a way to "borrow" this from the Bible and introduce the cinematic experience to the world.

Now, I want to tell you why I shared this story with you. As I end this first book in this series, I need to finish it here, with some thoughts and confessions on my own personal interaction with this bit of God's Word.

For several weeks I kept hearing about skeletons and dry bones. I read devotions which referenced them. I heard little kids singing, "Them bones, them bones, them dry bones." I heard worship songs from two contemporary Christian bands with lyrics about these bones. I came to the book of Ezekiel in my daily Bible reading as well. It seemed imperative that I take a look at this story in a personal way, so I did.

I prayed and asked God to speak to me through this vision. And wow, did He ever!

The first place that I heard God questioning me was at the part where He asked Ezekiel if he believed that the bones could live. The prophet answered that only God knew for sure. I think I had convinced myself that was my answer too. I would just brush over the question and read on as if I had that kind of crazy faith that God could do anything. I like to say that I do and think that I do, but when I felt God prompting me to answer Him, when I heard Him ask, "Amanda, can these bones live?" I knew that deep in my heart I had to respond with "No." It was as if I was being honest with myself for the first time.

Suddenly, I knew that the valley of dry bones was in my own heart. God began to show me that although I had amazingly beautiful mountain top places and streams of fresh water lined on both sides with leafy green trees grounded by thick deep roots, that there was a valley. The valley was so deep in my heart that if I drew a heart as a toddler would, it would be at the very bottom point, at that beautiful little place where the two soft rounded halves of the heart join together. At that sharp point was a barren valley, and it was filled with dry bones.

So the hand of the Lord was on me, and He brought Me there by His spirit, and he set me right in the middle of the valley which was full of dry bones. He had me walk back and forth among them. I saw them and began to realize what they had once been. This was the very floor of my heart, the things that I haven't looked at for years.

Dead and dry places. Here in this valley, all that are left are bones. These skeletons in my closet, these things I can't even recognize anymore, had been left there to turn to dust. And God asks, Amanda, can these things live? What I should say is, "only You know Lord," but what I have been saying to myself all of these years is, "No. They are dead. They are dry. They are bones. No, they cannot live."

But then God tells me to speak to the bones. He tells me what He declares to the bones, to these dead things in my life, to the valley things that have been trampled down by everything else going on around me, even good things. Then the Lord said He would make breath enter me, and I would come to life. He promised to attach tendons and cover my bones with skin, and bring me to life. So I spoke as I was commanded and it came to pass.

When we do what we are told to by God, even when it looks impossible, if it is the word of the Lord, it will come to pass. And then God said speak to the breath because even if it looks alive without the breath of the Lord, it's not.

God knows that my dry bones, the things in my valley, the stuff that's been underfoot since before I became a Christian, the things that I have hidden away deep down in my heart that I didn't want anyone else to know about, are there. He knows that they're dry, and He wants to bring them to life. God doesn't want to bring them to life to push me or to make me feel uncomfortable. He wants to bring them to life and put breath in them. And God wants them to become a vast army. And I think what He is saying is that those places that we are so sure are dead, we are sure are unrevivable, that those are the places that He wants to bring to life and send into action. The reason the bones were given tendons and flesh and breath are so that they can move out like an army.

So what if I were to take all of those things that I thought were too broken to fix, and what if God were to tell me to believe Him and to command those things to come to life in His name and what if He was able to do it? And what if those were the things that marched out from my heart and conquered the enemy? What if I connected with other people who had dry bones? He says that He is doing all of this so that we will know that He is the Lord. None of us could do this on our own. His heart is to bring those things to life. His heart is to add tendons and muscles and skin and to breathe His very life into it. That we would stand and walk together as a vast army. What if we all came to life and then went out into the world and helped others? What if we all connected in our dry and broken, places? What if we helped each other up off of the valley floor? What if we were meant to be fully alive?

After writing this all down, I had a vision of my own. I had drawn in my journal a skeleton, and then a person fully clothed with skin, and then I drew the breath of God entering them. I closed my eyes and listened for God, and what I saw in my mind's eye as I sang a worship song was this, I saw my resurrected being beginning to walk away from my valley of bones. As she walked, some skeleton hands and arms from skeletons that had not listened to the words spoken to them suddenly reached out and grabbed her around her ankles. They were like bony shackles that were trying to keep her in the valley. As I sang over the image trusting in who God is, I declared that chains must break in God's presence, and the skeleton arms broke off, and I was released to walk away, to leave the valley behind me, to move forward reborn and renewed!

Will you come with me?

I want to offer something unheard of. If you have read this book and you need to talk with someone if you have questions or you just are broken and don't know where to start with your healing I want to speak with you. I have created an email address: amandaspeaks11@gmail.com where you can contact me. I promise that I will respond to you. We are even considering creating an online community where we all can connect with each other in the future. This would be a place where we would be able to encourage one another. This book is the first of a series that will share my broken places and help you consider yours. My hope is that through describing how God has helped me heal, that you might find help healing also. This is the beginning of something, not the ending. Take the step to reach out and connect. I hope that you will be willing to see the amazing things that happen when you're willing to share your broken pieces.

THE BEGINNING...

CONCLUSION

It is more difficult than you would imagine deciding where to end a book. It is just as much a challenge as determining where to start. The concept of this book was to share my experiences with others and to draw them into my life to connect with them. That is a scary thing to do. These days it seems that everyone is a critic. But I have met too many people who do not understand that God loves them to not put this book out there. Some people have never heard that they don't need to get better, or clean up their messes, or become perfect before God wants to have a relationship with them. God already loves them. He already loves you. God loves you more than any human being ever can.

If you happen to be one of those people who has not yet experienced the loving relationship of God as Father, then it would be wrong of me not to add this final section to the book. If I am supposed to care about you, and I do, how would I not include the most beautiful news you will ever hear?

Maybe there are things in your life that have made it a struggle for you to understand God as a Father. Maybe your earthly Dad was absent, or abusive, or unloving. Perhaps you grew up desperately needing a Father, but no one was there to protect you, to provide for you, to teach you, or to support you. Many people have that kind of experience.

Maybe it wasn't your Father, but another family member or "friend of the family" who hurt you. I had a traumatic childhood. My parents were terrific but life happened to me, and I was wounded. I carried my brokenness around on my shoulders, slouching beneath its weight. I withdrew from intimacy with others, and I was anxious, frightened, and overwhelmed. I was codependent and had no idea how to draw a healthy boundary line. I was drowning in my sorrow and depression. I had become numb.

Over the years I made mistakes and decisions that have repercussions that might be with me for the rest of my life. I used drugs, alcohol, and sex as an escape from the internal suffering that had become so heavy that it was hard even to breathe. I had pushed my feelings down so far that I had no idea how to get better. It felt impossible for my life ever to change. Sleep became my best friend. Depression isolates you and then tries to kill you. I did whatever I could to escape from the pain.

My family went to Church, but what I experienced there were men and women trying to be "Godly." They didn't intend to give me such a poor impression of who God was, but they did. Instead of feeling the draw to His kindness and love for me, I felt ashamed as the Pastor's words were spoken from the pulpit. I would never be good enough for God to love me, I thought. That was a lie, but it was the very lie on which I would build my life. It became the foundation for my identity. I believed that it was the truth. I was wrong.

One evening, I encountered Jesus and my life completely changed. All of the shame that had kept my head looking down He lifted, gently raising my eyes to look into His. I didn't meet Him at a Church; I was in my own home. At that moment I had been busy excusing myself from a selfish and greedy thought, one that I assured myself wasn't bad at all. I felt that twinge of my conscience nudging me and the pit of my stomach felt queasy. Most days I would just ignore them both and move on, but at that moment something strange happened, I saw my greed and I knew that it was wrong.

All of the white lies, the complaining, the anger, anxiety, bitterness, escape, all of it was wrong. It was as if suddenly a menu of my favorite escapes was rising from my heart and I could see what had been hiding for so many years. Something radically twisted at that moment, as quickly as a head turning to see what made that awful crashing noise.

That part of my heart suddenly looked away from itself, and it turned towards something else, towards Someone else. It turned towards Jesus. It was at then that I realized the voice I had heard was His voice. He was with me.

I felt convicted, not persecuted or assaulted, but keenly aware of the knowledge that I had done something wrong. I was for a brief moment, surrounded by truth. Jesus was with me, and suddenly I knew that He loved me. I knew that I needed to admit that I had been wrong. I knew that I needed to be with Him. Jesus had been there all along, waiting for me to hear Him, to acknowledge His presence. That day I expressed my belief that He was there and that He was God. I thanked Him for going to the cross in my place. I realized that because of Him, I could come back into the family of God. I knew that I was a sinner. I knew that I needed what He died to offer me.

As my heart accepted who He was, suddenly I knew who I was — a wave of peace and love that is impossible to explain flooded me. I felt free. I felt the weight of my sorrow falling off of my shoulders. I could breathe. It was as if I was getting a massive hug as a warm strength enveloped me.

If anyone tells you that you need to be in Church to accept Christ as your Lord and Savior, they are wrong. God knows when our hearts are ready for the truth. And He waits patiently speaking that truth every day, every moment, every second of your life. The Bible says that Jesus stands at the door of your heart and knocks. Only you can let Him in. Don't be fooled, He could enter anytime that He wanted to, but to receive Him as Lord and Savior, you must willingly let Him in. To open the door, you must realize that He is God. God made a way to take our place and reconcile us back to Himself.

When Jesus agreed to come to make a way back into the family for us, He experienced every kind of situation that we do here on earth. Jesus felt every type of feeling and emotion that we have, but despite all of the unfairness and pain, Jesus never sinned. He always obeyed God's Will even the part that would send Him to die on a cross. He took our place. He loves you.

If you haven't read the Bible or attended a Church, this all may be new and confusing information for you. That is why I gave you my email address to contact me. I would love to answer any questions that you might have. What you need to know is that God loves you. He loves you just the way that you are. There is nothing that you need to do to get Him to love you. There is nothing that you have done that can keep Him from loving you. If you believe that, this is the most crucial time in your life! Getting into a right relationship with God will change everything.

When I allowed God His rightful place in my heart, my identity became His daughter. And as part of God's family, I immediately gained access to His kingdom. I have unlimited access to His presence which brings with it everything that I need. His presence brings love, protection, provision, peace, prosperity, wisdom, knowledge, purpose...this list is endless! But, I want to tell you that your life won't suddenly become perfect. There will still be plenty of tough circumstances and challenges ahead, but you will not face them alone. You will never be alone! Jesus will walk with you, carrying your burdens, lightening your load and pouring His peace and love into your heart. You will become an entirely new creation!

Before I asked Jesus to be in charge of my life, I was an introvert, anxious and quiet, nervous and timid. People who know me now have trouble believing that is true. I am always talking, super social and full of joy and energy. It seems every year that my heart is growing more youthful and active no matter what my outside is doing. I have opened up like a flower. Have you ever seen a Peony? It has one of the fullest blooms there is. Those flowers are stuffed with petals. I heard an interesting thing about them.

It seems Peony buds have some trouble opening and there is a specific kind of ant that loves to chew along the hard green scales that keep their buds closed. The ants gnawing is the thing that loosens the buds enough for them to open. Now that is a beautiful picture. The very thing necessary for us to bloom are the gnawing little pests of life that come along to disturb our peaceful isolation. I was as that bud, closed off, insular and withdrawn. The things that had happened to me had eaten at my soul, but like the ants, they had also loosened the hold that trauma, depression, and lies had on me. Without the brokenness, without the pain, without the suffering, I would never have become who I was meant to be! I have bloomed, and there is no way to ever stuff me back into my shell. I am fully open and the vibrant person that I was always intended to be.

Do you need what Jesus offers you? Are you tired and overwhelmed and feeling alone? There is a hole in our hearts and we don't realize that is where God was meant to reside. We try to fill it with things from the world. But stuff from the world can't fill it.

I am going to ask you to pray along with me. You can talk out loud or say this in your heart, God can hear you. But you must mean what you say. This prayer expresses your desire to trust Jesus for your salvation. Join with me saying something like this: "Jesus, for too long I have kept you out of my life. I need you. I am calling out to you. I am tired of doing things my way. Help me to start doing things Your way. I now know that I cannot save myself. I am a sinner. I trust you to be my Lord and Savior. Fill the emptiness in me with Your Holy Spirit and make me whole. Lord help me to trust You. Help me to love You. Help me to understand Your ways. I turn from my sin to You. Thank you for bearing my sins and dying for me. I believe Your words are true. Come into my heart and be my Lord."

Congratulations and welcome to the family! I would love to help you find a local church that can encourage you. And you need to begin reading God's Word. If you need any assistance finding a church or getting the right Bible for you please contact me at www.amandaspeaks11@gmail.com

I would love to help you get connected.

And if you find after completing this book, that you think you would benefit from having someone to talk to who is a mental health professional, I will list my daughter's information here. She is a Therapist specializing in trauma, anxiety and faith. She would love to help you. We care about you.

Lauren Bittner at: 215-858-0066
            www.lauren1bittner@gmail.com

NOTES

Printed in May 2019
by Rotomail Italia S.p.A., Vignate (MI) - Italy